By Joseph Olsen

POETRY

Between Us & Imagination
24 Hours

BETWEEN US & IMAGINATION

BETWEEN US & IMAGINATION

New & Revised Poems

JOSEPH OLSEN

FORMATION PRESS
NEW YORK

Copyright © 2024 by Joseph Olsen

All rights reserved.

This book or any portion thereof may not be reproduced or used in any manner whatsoever without the express written permission of the author except for the use of brief quotations in a book review.

For information about special discounts for bulk purchases, please contact Formation Press sales: sales@formationpress.com

Printed in the United States of America.

ISBN 978-1-7335450-3-7

Formation Press
Hudson Valley, New York
www.FormationPress.com

For You, Reader,
My Brother, My Sister, My Watcher, My Teacher.

CONTENTS

Preface - On Examining The Completed Work   /   18

from **Affixed to Heartbeat**

Affixed To Heartbeat   /   25
Re-Genesis   /   26
On The Boardwalk   /   28
All Things   /   29
Eden's Green Grass   /   30
Whom He May Devour   /   31
Hook, Line, And Sinker   /   32
Crashing Down   /   33
I Am Humming To You   /   34
Our Names Into Midnight   /   35
God Refuses   /   36
What Am I And Who Were You   /   37
It Never Ends   /   38
Halfway To Heaven   /   39
Today I Walked Through The Streets Of This City   /   40
Trying To Find Me   /   41
Little Hands   /   42
Prose For My Sweetheart   /   43
A Struggling Sun Seeks To Shine   /   44
I Scatter My Thoughts   /   45
The Cry Of My Body For Completeness   /   46
The Daises Wait In Seed   /   47
We Spend Our Lives   /   48
My Mind Wanders And The Pen Follows   /   49
A Pen, A Poem   /   50
He Walked Her Into My Life   /   51
Struggle Not   /   52
To You There's A Poem To Tell   /   53
With All I Write   /   54
Heart   /   55
By Her Kiss   /   56

from In Death, There Are Bones, No Fish

In Death, There Are Bones, No Fish / 61
Watering His Garden / 62
Biting Your Tongue / 63
I Gotta Go / 64
What Song / 65
Grand Central Bound / 66
Staring Down At Manhattan / 67
I Feel More Mature Than I Did Yesterday / 68
I Sit In Meditation / 69
Onto The Paper / 70
White Rabbit / 71
I Am Eager / 72
Against It All / 74
This Morning It Began To Snow / 75
The Old Man / 76
I Will Never Read This Poem Aloud / 77
Every Stroke Of The Midnight Hour / 78
Under The Weight Of Heartache / 80
I Endeavor To Encompass Infinity / 81
A Halo Of Neon Red / 82
Within This Poem / 83
The Child Within / 84
My Features Are Sharp / 85
An Epidemic Is Upon Us / 86
Pernicious Pillows / 88
An Hour Before The Clock Radio / 89
Another Page Crumbles / 90
They Claim They Know / 91
No Other Romance / 92

from **A New Day, A New Life**

A New Day, A New Life   /   97
Need To Know   /   98
I Hear The Clock   /   99
The Less Death Can Steal   /   100
In Love Again   /   101
First Steps   /   102
We Practice Waving   /   103
From The Darkness Of My Youth   /   104
Desperate Hands   /   105
Poetic Accolades   /   106
All Night   /   107
Through To The Afterlife   /   108
Read This Poem   /   109
Pen And Stacks Of Paper   /   110
Monkeys Know   /   111
Air Of Sophistication   /   112
Out Of My Head   /   113
Some Dead Poets   /   114
Love Remains   /   115
The Hush Of Night   /   116
The Eternal One   /   117
With Enough Rhyme.   /   118
Just Begun   /   119
La-Z-Boy Built For Two   /   120
On The World's Stage   /   122
Your Lifetime   /   123
Through Crowded Streets   /   124
Spiritual And Physical Worlds   /   125
Of Sacred Scriptures   /   126
Of The Two   /   127
The Death Of A Stray Horsefly   /   128
Worshiped By The Maddened   /   129
Midnight Seeds   /   130
Physical Expression   /   131
A Thousand Thoughts Expressed As One   /   132

New Poems

Between Us & Imagination   /   137
Dr. Allen Cut My Umbilical Cord   /   138
My Father's Favorite   /   139
My Father Was A Simple Man   /   140
One Of The Factory Worker's Sons   /   141
Life's Final Box   /   142
One In Ten   /   143
His Perspective   /   144
Plump, Jolly And Dressed For Dead   /   145
How To Entertain A Group Of Pigs   /   146
The Words I Write   /   147
Bleeding The Rose Its Red   /   148
I Can Hear Myself   /   150
Plead To Me   /   151
Departure From This Darkroom   /   152
Your Body Is In Your Soul   /   153
My Two Sons   /   154
Inspiration   /   155
Summer Ends   /   156
Same Name As A Dog   /   157
In Visible Forms   /   158
The Blue Trail   /   159
Caricature   /   160
Pinocchio   /   161
Poetic   /   162
Last Raindrop   /   163
I Refuse To Take Cover   /   164
I Have To Write   /   165
Consider Suffering A Spiritual Being   /   166
Our Hearts In His Hand   /   167
In Memoriam Thich Quang Duc   /   168
Meet Me   /   170
The Rodent   /   171
One, Two,, Three Tubes Of Blood   /   172
Inner Guide   /   173

Sunrise On The Shore   /   174
I Need You   /   175
As Their Creator Did   /   176
Hello, Hello Again   /   177
Spring Has Sprung   /   178
All Colors   /   179
The Meal   /   180
Under The Big Top   /   181
Too Naive To Think   /   182
Story To Tell   /   183
Panic And Pain   /   184
The Words Of The Prophets
Are Written On The Subway Walls   /   185
Proof Of Zen   /   186
Territorial Geese   /   187
The Stranger   /   188
The Imprint Of A Bird In The Sky   /   189
The Man In the Mirror   /   190
How Much I Love You   /   191
No Place To Hide   /   192
Undone (The Sweater Poem)   /   193
Not By Judgment   /   194
All Away   /   195
Indoor Water-Park   /   196
I Imagined Being A Third Grade Music Teacher   /   198
I Forgive   /   199
When I Grow Up   /   200
I Prayed   /   201
A Gorilla Escaped From The Zoo   /   202
As Below, So Above   /   203
Soft Kiss   /   204
From Heartbeat   /   205
Back Down   /   206
The Weight Of Mankind's Wickedness   /   207
At 44   /   208
The Deepest Love Of My Life   /   209
Basement Apartment   /   210
Decide   /   211

Honey Bee   /   212
Poetry   /   213
From Above   /   214
Not Wanting To Sleep   /   215

Acknowledgments   /   216

On Examining The Completed Work
Preface

"Lend yourself to others, but
give yourself to yourself."

-Michel De Montaigne

On Examining The Completed Work

I love quotes. From Michel De Montaigne to Tupac Shakur – on ambition, love, spirituality, war, and everything in-between. You will find them everywhere, scribbled on sticky notes adorned on the walls of my home, snapshotted on my phone, and penned in journals from reading poetry, novels, essays, reference books, and eavesdropped conversations that I've collected over the years.

Quotes force me to pause and reflect, making me want to be a better human and in early 2023 on a trip to Manhattan one made me a better writer.

Visting the New York Public Library's flagship location on Fifth Avenue, I sat journaling for a few hours in the majestic Rose Main Reading Room. The room is roughly the length of two city blocks – with a 52-foot-tall ceiling displaying murals of vibrant skies and billowing clouds. When I was done, I browsed the new gift shop and purchased a pocket edition of *The Elements of Style*, by William Strunk, Jr. and E.B. White. Eager to familiarize myself with the most influential grammar guide in the English-speaking world, I flipped to a random page and read something that suddenly jolted me. I copied the quote painfully in my journal, then exited the building, descended the steps and admired the regal poses of Fortitude and Patience (the library's two iconic marble lions on either side of the steps). I took a deep breath, leaned against Fortitude and gave the quote a star, an exclamation point, then highlighted it. The text shined like a beacon behind the yellow. Not wanting to feel rejected, inadequate, and discouraged, I flipped back some pages to a quote by the famous wit, Oscar Wilde,

"Life is too important to be taken seriously."

I contemplated the quote with nostalgia, reminiscing youth and my start as a writer.

My childhood consisted of nine siblings, welfare, stray dogs, legions of cockroaches, a psychic mother, and an alcoholic father. Growing up on Westchester Avenue in the Bronx the only serious thing I did was write, introduced to stories of the dead when my mother invited ghosts into our apartment after one claimed to be her stillborn daughter, Lisa, on a Ouija board. Earthbound spirits became intrusive, possessive, and made the apartment very cold. In an attempt to ward off the spirits the board was broken in half and thrown into the trash, but they remained, following my mother around like baby chicks to a mother hen.

She gave in to their request for communication and replicated the Ouija Board by drawing them on the back of the blank pages of Bibles, using a soda top tab as a planchette (a heart shaped pointing device you place your fingers on that is then moved by the presence of spirits). Every afternoon when school was out and on most weekends, she pulled me into her room to discover what the spirits had to say. We sat for hours which felt like days by candlelight as the musky smell of incense filled the air with our fingers on the soda tab top moving from letter to letter, yes to no, or number to number when my mother asked a question.

A few months later she did away with all "talking boards."

"I'm psychic now," she proclaimed, "Spirits *come through* and guide me, endowing me with the power to *pick up things.*"

There were midnight trips to the cemetery searching tombstones that provided further *evidence* on who some the spirits were in flesh and the year they died.

I was eight years old when my writing journey began, imagining stories and poems of astral corpses haunting the living and spirits trying to fulfill their missions to ascend the heights of purgatory into heaven to live in everlasting peace. I also began journal writing which fostered me through childhood squalor and allowed me to dis-identify myself as a victim, especially when I was eleven and watched my father push himself up from the recliner, stagger out to his brown Suburban, and drive off in retreat of fatherhood.

When I finished a story or poem I moved on to the next piece. I deemed myself a *professional* writer, calling my first drafts final drafts. I found it easier to let ideas flow than to scrutinize them and figure out how to make them better, causing me to egotistically publish three books of poetry in my twenties and early thirties, *Affixed to Heartbeat, In death, There Are Bones, No Fish,* and *A New Day, A New Life.*

When I returned home from the library that day, I flipped back to Strunk and White's quote, forcing myself to consider every word,

"Few writers are so expert that they can produce what they are after on the first try. Quite often you will discover, on examining the completed work, that there are serious flaws in the arrangement of the material, calling for transpositions...Do not be afraid to experiment with your text!"

I pulled my books of poetry from the book shelf and spread them out on the floor, picking up Affixed to Heartbeat. I flipped through it, examining the completed work. There seemed to be "serious flaws," not calling, but screaming for "transpositions." I picked up In Death, There Are Bones, No Fish. I flipped through it and had the same thoughts. A New Day, A New Life was no different. I felt even more rejected, inadequate, and discouraged, petrified of the text.

I then picked up my journal and opened it to a quote I copied from one of America's greatest and most original poets of all time, Emily Dickinson,

"After great pain, a formal feeling comes."

A few nights of nightmares and cold sweats ensued before a "formal feeling" numbed me. This absence of feeling became the inception of *Between Us & Imagination*. I embraced the void and took the three previous collections of poetry and selected poems to revise, looking for ways to improve clarity, stanza structure, and overall effectiveness. I cut back, contemplating a quote by Pamela Erens;

"In my experience, cutting back is the crucial act that allows the vitality, precision and emotional heart of a piece of writing to emerge."

Revising had become my favorite part of writing, making the selected poems from previous collections unrecognizable from their originals (which I have not bothered referencing).

I wrote new poems in the process of reworking the previous ones. Now in my mid-forties, I've fallen into the deepest love of my life and brought a little girl into this world, taking *Between Us & Imagination* to the next level.

These poems bring to mind a quote by Abhysheq Shukla, copied from a community chalk board in a café while I was on a three-day meditation retreat at a Buddhist Temple in Glen Spey, NY,

"Life is too ironic to fully understand. It takes sadness to know what happiness is, noise to appreciate silence, and absence to value presence."

I stare down at it now, give it a star, an exclamation point, and highlight it. The text shines like a beacon behind the yellow. I smile, feeling accepted, adequate, and encouraged, *knowing* what happiness is, *appreciating* silence, and *valuing* my presence which I hope invokes the same sentiments in you.

Joseph Olsen
Hudson Valley, New York
April 2024

from Affixed To Heartbeat
2005

"My pen beats faster
as I write with my heart"

—Munia Khan

Affixed To Heartbeat

Up there in his infinity
God's playing His favorite songs

Man and Woman
Drummed into existence

Loud and concrete
You and me
Affixed to heartbeat

No time, no resistance
No beginning to outdistance

No serpent, no resentment
No ending to reinvent

Up there in heavenly awe
God's dancing to His favorite songs
Infinity complete

Loud and concrete
You and me
Affixed to heartbeat

Re-Genesis

This vast
Aroused universe
Is in the moment
Of thawed winters
Into paradise springs
Eve puckers her lips
Adam moves in for the kiss
Mankind endures a re-genesis

Those who forget
Lay down to sleep
Dreaming of now
In the past
Waking tomorrow
At the light of dawn

Dead to flesh
Breath in man
Woman in seed
Beckoning the virgin sea
Here in this horny universe
Of conscious thought

Those who remember
Rise up from sleep
In future breath
Rousing the past with now
Present and profound

Sun and moon are in love
Wedded by nature's
Relationships
Sky directs
Mountains erect
Wind softly blows

Trough this vast
Aroused universe
In the moment
Of thawed winters
Into paradise springs
Eve puckers her lips
Adam moves in for the kiss
Mankind endures a re-genesis

Boardwalk

As a child's moon loomed in the firmament
Above the marshy ground below
On the boardwalk
A seagull gawked
Professing our love
We embraced by the shore
    You were sure

        I was more

On that splintery
Promenade
With bare feet
Treading lightly
    As God on high

        Whispered our soul names

On that creaky walkway
Reinforcing our existence
As grains of sand
Fully a man
    Fully a woman

        Universally one

As a child's moon loomed in the firmament
Above the marshy ground below
On the boardwalk
A seagull gawked
Professing our love
We embraced by the shore
    I was sure

        You were more

All Things

Sun, moon, and stars
Provide poetic ambiance
To my eternal soul
Confined as a human being
Experiencing all things
Perishable

Eden's Flowers Grow

We are the creators
Garden of words
Penned for love
In passionate prose

Look how Eden's flowers grow
Eden's flowers grow

Rooted in darkness
Through the soil
Into the light
Of heaven's eternal meadow

Oh, how Eden's flowers know
Eden's flowers know

In knowledge of the rose's red
We are prairies of wisdom
Yet shall we, though we were dead
In stable pose

Wow! How Eden's flowers glow
Eden's flowers glow

We are God's
Garden of words
Penned for love
In passionate prose

Look how Eden's flowers grow
Eden's flowers grow

Whom He May Devour

Mouse scrolls
Dog barks
Mouse clicks
Dog whimpers
Monkey's sober
Lion sleeps

Mouse clicks
Dog whimpers
Mouse scrolls
Dog barks
Monkey's vigilant
Lion roars
Walks about
Seeking whom he may devour

Hook, Line, And Sinker

Such an easy fish to catch
You stray from being a nobleman
From being a free thinker

Enticed by pride
You hope to gain respect
Nibbling on vain glory

Suduced by greed
You forget your hands are full
Ignoring the realm of the spiritual

Beckoned by lust
In dim-witted sensation
You commit simple fornication

Decieved by envy
You desire your neighbor's side
Where the illusion of greener grass lies

Courted by gluttony
You forget your belly's full
Over indulging, sleeping in rags

Hypnotized by anger
You call God an enemy
Solidifying Satan's supremacy

Recruited by laziness
You're reluctant to pray
Lax on today, yesterday

Such an easy fish to catch
You stray from being a nobleman
From being a free thinker

Hook, line, and sinker

Crashing Down

Angels of mercy
Let me

      Rest

In renewed innocence
In untethered flesh
                Rising
           Rising
      Rising

From such great heights
Angels of mercy
Let me

Come crashing
          Down

I Am Humming To You

I will not retire
Till the angels
Take my place
Relinquishing me from this human race
A thought today, a memory tomorrow
Competing with a new moon

In primordial tune
I am humming to you

Resonating energy of the universe
Replicating the rush of nature
Becoming a righteous creature
Sought to follow

In a melody of sorrow
I am humming to you

The soundtrack
To slumber's illusions
Dreams vibrating
The passing night
One with the flow

All I know
I am humming to you

I will not retire
Till the angels
Take my place
Relinquishing me from this human race
A thought today, a memory tomorrow
All the way through

I am humming to you

Our Soul Names

Carving our soul names into midnight
Retracing an angel's heavenly flight

Invoking remedies
For our physical inconsistencies

Consequently there will be me
Loving you

Beholding the beauty of celestial fame
Enjoying grace in humble acclaim

Under a silver moon with renewed love
A spark of the stars above

Calling out our soul names at midnight
Retracing an angel's heavenly flight

Invoking remedies
For our spiritual inconsistencies

Consequently there will be you
Loving you

God Refuses

God refuses to pay your rent
Not a single cent
Despite your egoistic faith in angels chiseled
On tombstones in the graveyard
God refuses to bestow to you in a nightly dream
The seven numbers needed to win the mega millions jackpot
God refuses to turn to Jesus
And suggest your luck change
Despite a nation you claim is yours
God refuses to rage war
And ship you off shore
God refuses your corporate enslavement of thirty years
To lay you off over a steep ledge
God refuses to pack up and leave like a deadbeat
Father to ten children
Despite your egoistic allegations of His abandonment
He paid your spiritual debt
To Satan, in satisfaction for the bondage and debt on the
Souls of humanity as a result of inherited sin
By the ransom sacrifice of Christ

What Am I And Who Are You

What am I
And who are you pretending to be?
The only one who can answer
Is righteous
Grand
God

What am I
And who were you a lifetime ago?
Sunset desires an audience
But we are
Slowly succumbing to eternal rest

What am I
And who were you last Sunday morning?
Bicycles built for two
Riding toward the promised land
With baskets full of daily bread

What am I
And who are you pretending to be?
The only one who can answer
Is righteous
Grand
God

It Never Ends

It never ends
Time of love transcends
Feeling and emotion
Or no time at all

It never pretends

Pasts malnourished with
Sunsets and break-aparts

It never lies

Nourished by it
We see with our single that

It never depends
On history or war
Or the tally of our ego keeping score

It never contends

Futures nourished with
Sunrise and get-togethers

It never ends
Time of love transcends
Feeling and emotion
Or no time at all

Halfway To Heaven

The ocean waves
An immortal soul

In a sailboat
Gaining distance
God is blowing kisses

A scene marveled
With opened eyes
One with the ocean's eternal now

Soft sand
Accompanied by a delicate breeze

Reciting poetry
From the swim of angels

Ceaseless
As the moment
Is fleeting

While seagulls crave
The ocean waves
An immortal soul

In a sailboat
Gaining distance
God is blowing kisses
Halfway to Heaven

Today I Walked Through The Streets Of This City

Today I walked through the streets
Of this city
In lower talk
With my higher self

Courtship in favor
Of an angel's reminisce
Block after block
Verse rolled off my tongue
And through my lips

Past Broadway's limelight
A stray
Between heaven and hell
Wandering dreary avenues of duality
With no name
In no fame

Walking through the streets
Of this city
In lower talk
With my higher self

Courtship in favor
Of an angel's reminisce
Block after block
Verse rolled off my tongue
And through my lips

Find Me

In the shadows of duality
His light is trying to find me

There is no temple
Without the body
In a world of form
Where everything weighs me down

There is no creator
Without the body
In a world of emptiness
Where everything
Is God

His light is trying to find me
In the shadows of duality

Masterpiece
For Tyler

His small eyes widen
His drawing hand in a frenzy
Back and forth across the page
The toddler doodles
Understanding
There's no-thing to understand
There are no rules
When you are innocent
No pressure
No limits to color
Within the lines

Holding up his doodle
The toddler's small smile widens cheek to cheek
A star-like twinkle in his eye
As I imagine, Van Gogh had
When he created his
Very first masterpiece

Prose For My Sweetheart

Journals bound with
Records of my existence
In black for
Those I've mourned
In green for
The rose's thorn

Journals heavy with
Meditations on the spiritual world
In gray for
The souls' essence
In white for
Gods' omnipresence

Journals swell with
Ruled indignation
In blue for
The suffocating page
In charcoal for
Midnight's rage

Journals age with
Rough drafts of the past
In violet for
Child's play
In gold for
The luxury of a sunny day

Journals bulge with
Prose for my sweetheart
In yellow for
The shedding of her favorite dress
In red for
The kiss of her succulent lips

Last Raindrop

After the rain fell
A rainbow
Arched across the sky
I marveled its beauty
Asking myself who I really
Wanted to be and nobody
Came to mind, but me

The rainbow disappeared
Like a fleeting thought
Its wavelength as long as the attention
Span of the last raindrop considered
Before questioning my existence

Awakened

The Cry Of My Body For Completeness

Do sun and moon transfigure each other
When they meet at dusk and dawn?
Am I really
Good and evils' natural spawn?
With worn fingertips
Is it worth hanging on?
In this darkness
Should I wait for the lights to come on?
Who does the red rose
Bloom upon?
Will Heaven or Hell
Endure continued success?
Love
Do you appreciate
The cry of my body
For completeness?

Daises Wait In Seed

Daisies wait in seed
As I wait in need
My love's fragrance left behind
In the bed
The sheets
On her pillow

Impatient and reckless
A lotus in muddy waters
Without her
As daisies wait in seed
Nourished by the sun above
I wait to be nourished by her

We Spend Our Lives

We spend our lives
Raising voices
Praying for God
To narrow down our choices
Untying our worldly tangles
In recent times
In impulse of childhood notions

We spend our lives
Forgetting who we are
Praying for God
To shower us with miracles
Quieting down our critical inner voices
In historic times
In impulse of childhood motions

We spend our lives
Remembering the lie
Praying for God
To be merciful
Judging our lives
In future times
In impulse of childhood archives

We spend our lives

My Mind Wanders and the Pen Follows

My mind wanders
And the pen
Follows

Through serene meadows
Angels are dancing to heartbeat
Saints are singing heavenly
Verse of warm yesterdays
On frigid tomorrows

My mind wanders
And the pen
Follows

A Pen, a Poem

A pen, a poem
I am home
A poem, a pen
I roam again
In bleeding, in red
Remembering the dead
In red, in bleeding
Needing to be read
A poem, a pen
Home I am
A pen, a poem
Again I roam

He Walked Her Into my Life

The poetry in my head was
On its tippy toes
Gazing over a high ledge
Ready to take the fall
I lacked much emotion
Parched of sentiment
On auto pilot with absentminded verse
God knew my poetry couldn't plummet
The depths of the dead

So He walked her into my life
Like he did to Adam with Eve
A yellow flower of Eden
Her long stems and sunlit smile
Imbued me with emotion
Returning my heart
To the center of all that mattered
Stepping back from that high ledge
My poetry rejoiced in love

Alive
So Alive!

Poetic

God's divinity is what ignorance
Conceals from midnight
In spiritual focus on the stars above
With all their light

With poetic eyes
Educated by prose
Of poetic sights

Each verse
Composed to be
You and me and love
Sweet love

Awakened ones are
In angelic posession
Of absolute truth
In spiritual comprehension

Poetically endevouring to
Inspire poetic converse
Pen to page
Of poetic rehearse

Each verse
Destined to manifest
You and me and love
Sweet love

To You There's a Poem to Tell
Sea Isle City, NJ

God's whispering in the crest and trough of a wave
Through a window of a vacation house
By the sea

Splendid thoughts matter in their fixed vibration
To a mind built well
To you there's a poem to tell

Days aren't spent in hell
Heaven is now
By the sea

In spiritual ruminations
Emotion sinks and swells
To you there's a poem to tell

God's whispering in a landward blowing breeze
Through a window of a vacation house
By the sea

His starry eyes gaze below
The perfect decibel
To you there's a poem to tell

With All I Write

The laces of my sanity
Knotted in foresight
Praising the blessed day
Under the sun's golden light
With all I write
Sparking heartbeat to ignite
Intense emotion
Contemplating mortality
Meditating on
Life's finality
The laces of my sanity
Untangled in hindsight
Praising the blessed night
Under the moon's silver light
With all I write

Heart

In optimal working order.
Sixty to
A hundred beats
Per minute.
Expanding and
Contracting
A hundred thousand times
Every 24 hours.
The size of a closed fist
But can be filled indefinitely
With bonds
To other beings.
Located in the center
Of all that matters.
Has mended from
Failed relationships
With no noticeable
Cracks.
Will continue beating
Until my body
Gives up the ghost.

By Her Kiss
For Amy

The day ended without her light
My body lifeless in the dead of night
Resurrected by her kiss
Sunrising upon our morning bliss

I was one of those sinners
Pleading to the heavens for a renewed heart
An imperfect man deserved a muse
I deserved her poetry

Disenchanting sleepless nights
Regretting the push of ego
I closed my eyes to her beautiful sight
Her golden glow

The day ended without her light
My body lifeless in the dead of night
Resurrected by her kiss
Sunrising upon our morning bliss

from In Death, There Are Bones, No Fish
2008

"The reason we want to go on
and on is because we live in
an impoverished present."

-Alan Watts

In Death There are Bones, no Fish

In death there are bones
No fish

Up the long stairs of heaven
Of white floor boards
And perfect, uncontaminated nails

No water
No rivers that lead to the seven seas
No-seed to accomplish

In death, there are bones
No fish

Through life
In cemeteries
Silent as the dead sleep

No breath without a gust of wind
No gust of wind without
A child's wish

In death there are bones
No fish

Down the short stairs of hell
Of ash floor boards
And dull, rusty nails

No water
No rivers that lead to the seven seas
No-seed to accomplish

In death there are bones
No fish

From One End of Heaven to the Other

God watered His garden
Falling rain on Earth

From one end of Heaven
To the other
The angels opened
All the chambers of the stars

You'd of seen them
If all the clouds weren't
Obstructing your view

To What End

Losing the freedom
To offend
Biting your tongue
But to what end?
The system lacks
The breath of life Godsend
Suffocating
You're unable to contend
Biting your tongue
But to what end?
Losing the freedom
To offend

I Gotta Go

She's running from her past
I must go
Where she's taking a breather
Contemplating unconditional love
Forging a soul
Out of time with each succesive footstep
She's running from her past
I must go
Where she's having a rest
And lay with her
Creating a new past
In the present

What Song

In my head
I tour a gallery of memories
Hanging like old photographs
In crooked, dusty frames
Wondering
What song could be
My eulogy

Grand Central Bound

In Beacon, NY
I board the Metro North
Commuter railroad just in time
To avoid a downpour
Rattling along the Hudson River
Grand Central bound
I watch millisecond lovers
With graffiti smiles
Kiss nine to five gurus
In three piece suits
Gaining distance, past Cold Spring, Croton-Harmon
Tarrytown, Yonkers, Harlem
Having finally arrived at Grand Central Terminal
I exit the train
Ascend the stairs to the atrium
Past the terminals iconic clock
I step outside just in time
To witness a sky full of clouds dissipate
As God's blaring sun
Welcomes me to the concrete jungle

Staring Down At Manhattan

I stare down at Manhattan through a window
On the tenth floor of a building
On 27th Street
Catching my reflection in the tempered glass
I notice features of my parents
And wonder how they squander their time
Do they ever catch their reflections
And notice me
Staring down at Manhattan through a window
On the tenth floor of a building
On 27th Street?

I Feel More Mature Than I Did Yesterday

I feel more mature
Than I did yesterday
Going 65
On the thruway
Sacred love emanating
From the heart bared on my sleeve
While a venerable golden retriever with no seatbelt
In the passenger seat of a jalopy
Sticks its head out the window
Feeling more mature
Than I did yesterday
Brainstorming last night's dream:
A journal penned with blood
Ripening reality
Ruminating a future of childlike innocence
Feeling more mature
Than I did yesterday
Slowing to 45
On the thruway
As a senior in the driver's seat of a jalopy
Signals for the off ramp of exit 17
While a venerable golden retriever with no seatbelt
In the passenger seat
Pants sacred love emanating
From the heart bared on the fur of its forelimb

Meditation

I sit in meditation
Like Buddha under the
Bodhi tree
Like Jesus on a sand dune in
The desert

Carrying my breath
Like carrying ghosts

Holding my breath
Like holding oaths

Humbly refusing the *ego mind*
It's expectations and desrires

Easing down
I plant
Divine seeds
Of freedom

Refraining from the desire
To witness their liberation

Sitting in meditation
Like Buddha under the
Bodhi tree
Like Jesus on a sand dune in
The desert

I Write

I write

From the mind
Into the pen
And onto the paper

Not who the televison programs

From the evening broadcats
Into the subconscious
Intruding the private space of ones unconscious

I write

From the mind
Into the pen
And onto the paper

White Rabbit

My mind is the White Rabbit
    Leading my pen
        Down the rabbit hole
            Of imagination

oh dear
OH DEAR!
I shall be too late For
ANYthing at all
        Writing away
           In
Wonder Land

I Am Eager

I am eager
I am mortal
I am the first day of creation

I am jazz, doo-wop
Classical, and rock 'n' roll
Bundled into one

I am the Peace Scene of the Standard of Ur
I am civilized in an uncivilized nation
I am eternal in the present moment
I am immaterial
I am the ripe fruit of original sin
I am forgiven

I am rock 'n' roll, doo-wop
And classical
When there is no jazz
Bundled into one

I am a combination of the four seasons
I am Jesus' last supper
I am the Alpha and Omega
I am enlightened verse of contemporary poets
I am alive in the dead of night

I am jazz, doo-wop
Rock 'n' roll
When there is no classical
Bundled into one

I am dressed in black
I am overcome
I am in love
And out late
I am an illusion
I am free booklets of unbridled faith

I am jazz, doo-wop
And classical
When there is no rock 'n' roll
Bundled into one

I am following the leader
I am the leader
I am the rain
And the shine
I am divine
I am going back for more

I am jazz, rock 'n' roll
And classical
When there is no doo-wop
Bundled into one

I am the last day of creation
I am immortal
I am eager

Against It All

Under a night of starlit fame
The mind aspires
The heart desires

Twilight hours
Typing a war
Against it all

Without thought
This verse is you
A perception of what's true

Winds to blow
The spirit
To carry on

So far undirected
The mind's in danger
Your heart's in anger

Lonely
Enduring emptiness
Wondering who you are

Dreaming unfortified
Your mind's to depart
Bless your beating heart

Under a night of starlit fame
Typing a war
Against it all

Two Inches Deep

It began to snow this morning
In the cemetery
Meditatively still
Inhaling almighty
I endured Winter's luxurious chill
Above empires below
Preserved in paradoxical sleep
Barren, breathless
Quiet beneath the falling snow
Exhaling omnisiently
I knew at any moment I could relinquish control
Constrained indefinitely with those in their plots below
Eight feet long
Two and a half feet wide
Six feet under the living
Meditatively still
Preserved in paradoxical sleep
As the morning snow accumulated
Two inches deep

The Old Man

The old man glares
At feminine and masculine
Beauties of youth
Grinning through pearly whites

Suffering pressure to the jaw
From spent dentures
Tested on physical commitment
A patient of patience

Habituated to routine
In arthritic observations
The old man glares
At feminine and masculine
Machines of God
Ignorant of original sin

He could try and
Talk of what used to be
Pass on knowledge of salvation
But what's the use?
How much water could
Feminine and masculine
Beauties of youth possibly draw
Grinning through pearly whites
Talking of what is now
In trending conversations
Competively loud
And obnoxiously arrogant

I Will Never Read This Poem Aloud

No verse through these lips will be heard
Not a single word
I will never read this poem aloud

Other poems should be read before I go
Ones you should know

Listening to heartbeat's play
Listening to what this poem will not say

As other poets perish before my demise
It's best no one hear my cries

Listening to the Valentines cupid turned his bow away
Listening to what this poem will never say

No verse through these lips will be heard
Not a single word
I will never read this poem aloud

The Midnight Hour

Lodged in this skin
Heartbeat drumming out my youth
Revealing truth

My inner child will never expire
Reborn at every stroke of the midnight hour

Arms around my soul
Embraced in this physical form
A summer breeze to and fro

Coloring the white rose red
Washing the wound of original sin
Closer to redemtion
I suggest you follow

Angels flying with the petals of a lotus flower
At every stroke of the midnight hour

Eyes on the stars above
Taming the ego within this spiritual form
Unknowing

Striking the arson's match
As no material belonging
Is worth any man's demise

A full moon shines with great power
At every stroke of the midnight hour

Staring down my demons
I will not turn away
Under a celestial night
Of heavenly might

Lodged in this skin
Heartbeat drumming out my youth
Revealing truth

My inner child will never expire
Reborn at every stroke of the midnight hour

Heartache

There is no one to believe
No love worth my trust
No innocence to skip heartbeats
Out of sequence with the divine
No reason to sleep
Mourning sunlight
Forced back by midnight
Unstable
Like a game of twister
Falling over my ego
Nothing to write
No words to define
The ineffable buckling
Under the weight
Of heartache

To Encompass Infinity

I endeavor to encompass infinity
Slipping through my fingers
Like the sands of time
One cannot grasp what the spirit yearns

I never wanted it more
Into the wind it took flight
The enlightened thought directing me
To where I am

I endeavor to beckon infinity
Its essence known to be
The heartbeat
Of creator

I never wanted it more
A miracle
Like a night of sparkling stars
No spirit will do better

I endeavor to replicate infinity
Making it all mine
Too good to be temporarily true
No spirit can do better

I never wanted it more
Like a ghost
Into the void
Feigning heartbeat

I endeavor to encompass infinity
Slipping through my fingers
Like the sands of time
One cannot grasp what the spirit yearns

Halo Of Neon Red

The yellow of my coward-ness
Shines like a setting sun
On a past not my own
But of the ego's
I will not be
Evicted from the temple

In the indigo of the present moment
I stand on the fertile soil of a future truly my own
Slaying my ego
Crowned with a halo of neon red
By God in his temple
Not built with hands

Within This Poem

Within this poem
Raw emotion

Without these stanzas
At a cafe, over a table
A father shares a blueberry muffin with his son

Within this poem
I cannot hold back the overt emotion

I'm without
Where blueberry muffin crumbs
And coffee stained napkins lie

Within this poem
Crude emotion lingers

Without these stanzas
At a cafe, standing at a table
A father embraces his son

Within this poem
I cannot hold back the rare emotion

I'm without
Memories of my father
Raising me

Within this poem
Raw emotion deepens

Without these stanzas
At a cafe, over a table
I absentmindedly grab a coffee stained napkin
And wipe away tears

Inner Child

He's staring out from
The depths of
Me
Believing nothing
Of what
I know
Wounded from *our* past
Challenged to resolute
Invocations of
Inner desires
Subjected to imperfection
Victimized by mental manipulation
He's staring out from
The depths of
Me

Thirty Three

I don't look as young
As I used to
My face isn't the face of the child I used to be
My features are sharp
My eyes are deep
On the surface of their orbits
A murder of crows have
Imprinted their feet

Dominated by the carnal mind
Biding my time
Passing judgment
To be
Or not to be
Wholeheartdly spiritual
Eternally thirty three
The age
Men of God
Are to sacrafice themselves

A Pandemic Is Upon Us

The population is impure
Our end is premature

Blood pools from fallen loves
Brushes dipped by aspiring Picasso's and Monet's
Crimson strokes across taught canvasses
Giving up their aspirations
They flee their masterpieces

Speeding through midnight
Truck drivers ain distance from
Health benefits and retirement savings
Passing brick and mortar vacancy
Right on up
To that perfect place of divine rest

Doctors practice medicine for the last time
Injecting water prescribed by shamans
From the fountain of youth
Into their veins
Rushing into helicopters to live forever
On fantasy islands

Postmen with wide eyes
Rummage through mailboxes for the letter
Their true love had sent

Thugs lay down their weapons
To help the elderly, patiently
Cross expressways

Teachers flee from their lessons and students
Into the embrace of doctors
To live forever on fantasy islands

The pope kisses the virgin
Bundles up the baby
And collects what is left
In those silver dishes
Packing his spaceship with papal artifacts
To live in paradise
On the outer rings of Saturn.

Writing as chaos ensues
Between midtown and uptown
New York
New York
A poet in a wife beater
Titles his poem,

A Pandemic Is Upon Us

Pernicious Pillows

Mother is out gallivanting
Her children are
Sleeping

Father is out drinking
His children are
Weeping

On pernicious pillows
Fluffed with darkness and squalor
Dreaming that holy scripture
Of being taken up

*When my father
And my mother
Forsake me,
Then the Lord
Will take me up.*

Mother is out gallivanting
Her children are
Weeping

Father is out drinking
His children are
Sleeping

On pernicious pillows
Fluffed with isolation and affliction
Dreaming that holy scripture
Of being taken up

*Psalm 27:10

An Hour Before The Clock Radio

You fret over a future
And a past that's never existed
Forgetting your dreams
Sleeping the stars away
And the sun
Which rose an hour before
The clock radio blared an oldie
But goodie
Jolting you from slumber
You collect everything of yourself
But your spirit
Left behind
In forgotten dreams

Another Page Crumbles

The vacancy of the wordless page
Beckons my mother
In-between the lines
She's searching for a place to hide
My inner child yearns for her attention
Craves being noticed
To be shown sunrise
Is to begin again

The nullity of the text-less page
Beckons my father
In the margins
He's stumbling over his past
My inner child yearns for his sobriety
Aches for his comprehension
To be shown sunset
Isn't to scrape by

My pen
Fumbles
Another page
Crumbles

They Claim

They claim you're destined
For heartache
Hating love
They claim it's best
To desire war, firing a gun
Killing all the flowers
They claim you're an average Joe
With a history of abuse
Lies solidifying your youth
They claim the avenues are littered with thieves
The streets are a chessboard
And you, an expendable pawn
They claim nirvana is materialism
An existence of the perfect glow
Dying the staus quo
They claim it's the hour
No time left
For redemption
They cliam God is ashamed of you
You who have
A mindful of stardust

No Other Romance
For Amy

Admiration exceeds its limits
Your flesh on my flesh
In poetic advance
No other romance stands a chance

Affection mends loneliness
Your chest I'm pressed against
In-sync heartbeat
No other romance is blessed

A disciple of true love, I am
Snuggled in your embrace
Face-to-face
No other romance can replace

Twin flames divine
Your love is a firestorm
In bodily form
No other romance can perform

Devotion exceeds its limits
Your flesh on my flesh
In poetic advance
No other romance stands a chance

from A New Day, A New Life
2010

"Man starts over again everyday,
in spite of all he knows,
against all he knows."

—Emil Cioran

A New Day, A New Life

Owning rented eyes
Marveling morning's rise
The sun so bright

A new day, a new life

The body is God's refuge
Evicting overdue egos
Heartbeating
The night's demise

Thoughts are God's imagination
Inviting Christ to mind
Shinning truth
On the night's lies

Owning rented eyes
Marveling morning's rise
The sun so bright

A new day, a new life

If You Want To Know

To explain
That I am no one
You'd ever need to know
Would do nothing to mend
Your lonely heart
But, if you
Want to know
A different
Kind of love
Please
Let me explain

The Still Ticking Clock

Behind the heavy antique dresser
With the faux crystal
Knobs
In that hard-to-reach place
The clock is still ticking

Thrown last Monday
At six a.m.
When I was expected at my desk
Of a dead end job

Now, Saturday morning
Pulling a fresh pair of socks
From the top drawer
I wonder
How long a double-A battery can last
And when the clock does finally stop ticking
Will I be working another dead end job?

Dream Journal

I
Wake up
With a new idea of
Who I used to be
Without looking at me
Subconsciously
I see my soul
Jesus in my chest
Christ in my head
Annointing me
Knowing
God
As I am
Never an idea of
Who I used to be

Actions Speak Louder

Two days and we are still distant
Alone
I sit in the kitchen
Lights dimmed
Irrational all-or-nothing phrases,
"You never..." or "You always..."
Echo off the walls of my mind
I try standing up again
This time it works
I walk to the bedroom
Stare at you in the door way
Lying sideways on the bed
Beautiful
A lone angel
And I want to tell you not to drop it
That you are not making a big deal over nothing
But the words do not come
And they don't matter
Because actions speak louder
I make haste across the threshold
Tripping over my broken heart
Into your embrace
In love
Again

First Steps
For Nicholas - October 11th, 2008

While homeless leaves
Scurry about the streets
October's sun
Shines through the living room window
As my son, in his tenth month
Of existence

Cawls to me
And grabs my pointer finger
His fragile grip
Like the remaining foliage
Clutching to Summer's trees
He pulls himself up
Onto his own two feet

Then, relinquishing his grip
He takes three steps
Out of a ray of light
October's sun shines forth

And as an Autumn breeze
Forces a fortune of leaves
To surrender to gravity

So does he

We Practice Waving
For Nicholas

The only weapons of mass destruction are propaganda
Pawning soldiers off across the sea
Father's are desperate and worn
A misinformed war's to be won

We practice waving hello
Me and my firstborn son

While soldiers ready their gun
I laugh along
Tickling my firstborn son

Prayers to God from our side
Prayers to God from their side
With angelic presence my eyes he does adorn
I kiss his forehead
Leaving slumber to entertain my firstborn son

The only weapons of mass destruction are propaganda
Pawning soldiers off across the sea
Father's are desperate and worn
A misinformed war's to be won

We practice waving goodbye
Me and my firstborn son

From The Darkness Of My Youth

I rise
Greeting the world with gospel truth
Sunlight manifested
From the sacrafice of my youth

Baby steps
Toward heavenly truth
Encountering God
From the comprehension of my youth

Every moment
Searching the season's truth
Known
From the retrospect of my youth

With innocence
Above worldly truth
Writing
From the pages of my youth

I sleep
Greeting my dreams with gospel truth
Moonlight manifested
From the dreams of my youth

Desperate Hands

A starving children ad aired on the television
But instead of neglected and
Malnourished children from third world
Contries
I saw me and my nine siblings
Huddled in our Bronx apartment in 1989
Our small, desperate hands
Reaching out
Begging for our fill

Poetic Accolades

Back and forth like a pendulum
I oscilate between envy
And being unfulfilled

Reading
A two-term United States poet laureate
Laugh at me between his lines

Then I arrange my own words
And emotions
Into poetry

Then back to reading
A pushcart prize winner
Scold me between her lines

I could enter the contests and potentially win
No longer judging myself
Against the success of others

But would I be satisfied
No longer an anxious inhabitant
Of the worried abode of my mind?

Up At The Stars

All morning I
Conversed
With Angels
Who proclaimed the stars
Were God's scars
Etched by the fall
Of each man
As reminders of
His unconditional love

With habitual assumptions
I claimed I understood it all
When the Angels chuckled
I knew I hadn;t
Understood nothing at all

Then dawn came
And the Angels ascended
And all night I
Looked up at the stars
Gainning wisdom
Marveling God's scars

Through To The Afterlife

When I journey from this physical dimension
To the afterlife
Through the pearly gates
Spotlighted by the glow of eternal glory
I will gather up
Our saviour, the saints, prophets
And holy ones of Heaven

Then before them
I will recite
A dead man's poetry

Read This Poem

There may be
Better things to do

The body of your love
Weightless. Waiting
Relentless

Television telling you to
Agree with the politicians
Get out of debt. Buy the pills
Order now!

There may be
Nothing better to do

The body of your love
Favorably dreaming
Volatile

Television muted, miming
Blah Blah Blah
Blah Blah
Blah

Pen And Stacks Of Paper

Beneath the stars
Writing
This infinite moment
Captivated by déjà vu
Counter clockwise
To a poem's inception
To an original thought
Heaven's stored treasure
Beneath the stars
Writing
This infinite moment
Beckoning my creator
With pen
And stacks of paper

Monkeys Know

Monkeys know
There's more than enough
To go around
But the human population
Lacks divine knowledge
Distancing themselves form the Angels
The humans entertain demons
In limited pleasure
They take turns medicating each other
With broken promises
They are at war
Desiring to control the future
In a one sided battle
Destroying nature
Polluting the seas

Obliterating
All the monkeys

Air Of Sophistication

This poem carries
An air of sophistication

I believe I am
Liberated more than
Most men in their forties
At their day jobs
Striving toward a comfy retirement

While I strive toward awakening
Painting sunlight with words
At my writing desk
Enduring mild back pain

Out Of My Head

I rose at midnight
Poetry itching to get
Out of my head

At my writing desk
I listen to poetry
Whisper heavenly secrets
Reciting verse of
The Cosmo's constellations

Back and forth across the page
Poetry's evolution transcribed
Onto the blank page

With well needed rest
I snuggled back into bed
Poetry itching to get
Out of my head

Some Dead Poets

I spent a snowy evening
Searching for Frosts' horse
Through perfect woods
Without a farmhouse near

Strapped into the roller coaster
Of free thought
I rode Ferlinghetti's
Coney Island mind

Poe's Annabelle
In my own
Love
I see

Like Bukowski
I met a genius
He asked if I could
Spare some change

Simic's Slaughterhouse Flies
Over the pages
Of my
Poetry

Summer days
With Shakespeare's eyes
I compare
Thee

Like Dickinson
I'm nobody
Are you nobody
Too?

Love Remains

Souls playing life's game are sure to fall from flesh
Cemeteries fill with the forgotten
Sunset is to blame
As love
Remains

Love
Remains

We who commit long to make ends meet
Valentine after valentine
Again and again
Cupid draws back his bow

Cupid draws back his bow
In perfect aim

Souls playing life's game are sure to fall from flesh
Cemeteries fill with the shells of the reborn
Sunset is to blame
As love
Remains

Love
Remains

Without Light

Adrenaline-rushed heartbeats
In the hush of night
There is darkness without light

No prose written
No future living
There is no thought without light

No heaven No hell
Only ghosts with no shame
Floating aimless in the crush of night

No verse to listen
No past remission
There is no cognition without light

No presence No being
Only stars with no names
Shooting aimless in the rush of night

No verse to listen
No past remission
There is no cognition without light

Only adrenaline-rushed heartbeats
In the hush of night
There is darkness without light

Eternal One

The floodgates of Earth's womb
Will open and we will
Leave this temporary place
Where the firmament holds the sun
Moon and stars
Our souls will merge
Giving birth
To the eternal one

Enough Rhyme

Enough rhyme bends time
Bathing in the moonlight of the ego's kill
Invoking the spirits will
Of love
Breaking all unworthy ties
Enough rhyme xposes worldly lies
Remembering what we've misplaced
Who we've lost
Waiting to be found in enough rhyme
The page

Just Begun

What is the insect's
Purpose?
So tiny
So insignificant
I cannot tell
Where it will fly
Like angels of light
Emnating celestial influence

La-Z-Boy Created For Two

Downstairs, Hollywood stages heaven
We act godless
Congregating fatherless

Upstairs, Jesus is expecting you
In a La-Z-Boy created for two

Downstairs, mirrors echo the dead
We fade away
Like promises from old loves

Upstairs, saints pride themselves
On immortality

Downstairs, innocence is questioned
By children impressed upon
Full grown anger

Upstairs, angels nurse newborn prophets
Above our golden sun

Downstairs, unconditional love is transient
Roadside church signs remind us that
Kneeling will leave us in good standing

Upstairs, St Nicholas is reading
In an armless lawn chair

Downstairs, man remains earthbound
While spirituality proclaims
Gravity can be overcome

Upstairs, souls stare down through
Glassless windows

Downstairs, the flames of time rage on
As the Phoenix rises
Again from its ashes

Upstairs, angels clear away
Smoke

Downstairs, Hollywood stages heaven
We act godless
Congregating fatherless

Upstairs, Jesus is expecting you
In a La-Z-Boy created for two

Start With Me

Your Lifetime

Their eyes are my eyes
Peering through my features
My senses, my senses, my smile
My countanace

Their lips are my lips
Puckering for my kiss
My desire, my defeat
My sacrafice

Their hands are my hands
Longing for my touch of luxury
My comfort, my palms
My fingertips

Their poems are my poems
Questioning existence
My verse, my stories
My fairy tales

Their thoughts are my thoughts
Reminiscing my youth
My fruit, my light
My seeds

Their years are my years
Winding down to days
My minuets, my seconds
My lifetime

Through Crowded Streets

Wandering through crowded streets
In furs and manufactured smiles
Congested in summer dresses and designer suits
Masquerading in masks and soft sole shoes
In temples of individual heartbeats
The blind are
Leading the blind
Searching for a savior
Through crowded streets

When I Grow Up

When I
Grow up
I will have
The innocence to still decipher
The permutations of the clouds
When I
Grow up
I will be outside the lines
Abandoning my comfort zone
Exploring rainfall
Half dressed, sopping wet
Dancing in laughter
When I
Grow up
I will defy time
And grow down
When I
Grow up

Reciprocating Smiles

One Of The Two

Louder and louder
Lovers shout
"Money's running out!"
One of the two made the bet
Gambled to be better set

Older and older
Lovers grow
Time dimming their glow
One of the two couldn't relinquish the past
Damned to be the first to last

Colder and colder
Lovers decay
Arguing in every way
One of the two considered the danger
Promised to control their anger

Night and day
Lovers woe
Letting go
One of the two craved enlightenment
Claimed entitlement

Memory after memory
Lovers see
Imagining what used to be
One of the two caved in
Uncomfortable in their skin

Louder and louder
Lovers shout
"Money's running out!"
One of the two made the bet
Gambled to be better set

The Death Of A Horsefly

It took the patience of a saint
Taking the life
Of a horsefly
Buzzing around my writing desk
One o'clock in the morning

While two elementary school boys
Lay fast asleep
Ignorant of the horsefly
Buzzing aimlessly. Buzzing erratically
Buzzzzzing, buzzzzzing, buzzzzzing!

Flying clear of my writing desk
And landing on the wall
A zenful silence ensued
As the horsefly rubbed its scrawny legs together
In a premeditated ascent of torture
Resuming its aimless and erratic buzzing
One forty five in the morning

That's when I assassinated the horsefly
With the swift swat of a compilation of American poetry
The two elementary school boys lying fast asleep
Bolted up from their dreams

Tears streaming down their faces
A eulogy for the aimless, non-erratic
Non buzzing horsefly
Two o'clock in the morning

Worshiped By The Maddened

"I form the light, and create darkness:
I make peace, and create evil:
I the Lord do all these things."
Isaiah 45:7

I'm broke
Mangled, disturbed,
A spiritual mess
And it was God who broke me
Adamant to be
Worshiped by the maddened

Midnight Seeds

Sunset
The ripe fruit of enlightenment
Down
To the
Pits

With insatiable desire
The soul of the master gardener
Cultivates thoughts from the dead
With fertile sight
In great deeds
Two eyes
From one vision
Mourn dawn

Moonset
The ripe fruit of knowledge
Pits
To the
Down

Physical Expression

I hear the ghosts
Fumbling in the dark
For the light
Strangers without mornings
Struggling to lift the veil and
Catch a glimpse
Of the rising sun

With other worldly hunger pangs
The ghosts are starving
For physical expression
I feed them
By reciting poems written
When I was young, invincible
Quick witted, blameless
And very much alive

Love Is

Between Us And Imagination
New Poems

"The creation of something new is not
accomplished by the intellect
but by the play instinct acting from
inner necessity. The creative mind
plays with objects it loves."

-C. G. Jung

Between Us And Imagination

Between us and imagination
God is suiting up souls
For this physical dimension

Experiencing years of life's duration
Fesh, blood and bone
Marveling streams over sun-kissed stone
Poetically contemplatiing
God's thirst for physical hydration

Tangibly existing
Confirming God's attention
Heads on chests in tune withf heartbeat
On spiritual relation
God's craving physical affection

Somatic persistence
Confirming God's physical intention
Flesh, blood and bone
Marveling streams over sun-kissed stone
In spiritual donation

God is suiting up souls
For this physical dimension
Between us and imagination

Dr. Allen Severed Me From My Mother

On April 15th, 1979
Dr. Allen announced
That I wasn't going to make to July
He cut my mother open
And pulled into the world

A two pound eleven ounce whimpering piece of flesh
Dr. Allen surveyed the room and concluded that
My father was in the basement on Westchester ave
Under a half-lit Bronx moon
Opening a fresh bottle of scotch alone
So, Dr. Allen cut my umbilical cord
Severing me from my mother

He then stitched her back together
Stealing any chance of me
Getting back inside
For those few months til July
Where (possibly) my father
Inebriated off the life of his newborn son
Would push Dr. Allen aside
And sever me from my mother

Father's Favorite

Father was a fertile man
His favorite woman to impregnate was my mother
Eight children were conceived
His least favorite woman to impregnate
Was his first wife
Three children were conceived

Father was a heavy hitter
His favorite punching bag was me
After a session of pounding my back, he'd turn away and
Smoke his favorite brand of cigarettes; Bel Air
Leaving an anvil on my chest
And a cocktail straw to breathe through

Father made paint for a living
His favorite things to spend his wages on
Were bottles of Dewar's Scotch
While his starved children
Anticipated sustenance that never came

Father was a handyman on the side
His favorite places to fix up were other people's homes
While our apartment's bathroom flooded
Legions of roaches scattered
And frayed floorboards pierced our feet

Father loved road trips
His favorite one was
Abandoning his favorite woman
And children he concieved with her
Like a thief robbing a bank
He packed his favorite belongings
Into his brown Suburban
And in *my* most cherished memory ever
I watched him drive off
In retreat from fatherhood

My Father Was A Simple Man

My father was a simple man
With elementary paint factory wages
He provided a destitute life for me and my nine siblings
At the end of the day he simply drank his scotch
And fell fast asleep on the floor

My father was a simple husband
With primitive emotions
He snuggled the neighborhood prostitute
In retaliation to the attentive men my mother smiled at
He simply couldn't comprehend
The complexities of love

My father was a simple teacher
With half-witted haste
He instructed me to give up
Before anything began
He simply couldn't cope with the consequences
Of competition

My father was a simple deadbeat
With ill-tempered patience
After 17 years of marriage
He seized the moment we were all sleeping and
Simply jumped into the driver's seat of his Suburban
And drove off to live out his lifespan

My father was a simple man

One Of The Factory Worker's Sons

I am one of the factory worker's sons
A concrete rose quenching my thirst
From the salty tears of poverty

One of the factory workers is my father
A dehydrated weed
Exhausted, slouched on a machine

Inhaling the dust of his wrinkling skin
He doesn't think of me, never thinks of God
He's forgotten us, forgotten we exist

He's bleeding
Quenching death's thirst from life's cold flow
He is a factory worker and I am one of his sons

How did I get so old?
Why am I at my threshold?

Life's Final Box

Life's final box
Lowered into
Pulverized rocks
Adorned with roses
Wilting around the plot

You frequent the lowered box
Intimidated by the clenched fists
Pulverizing the rocks
Waiting your turn
Adorned with silence
Suffering around the plot

In life's final box
The dead sleep
Indefinite hours
Their spirit ascends to the clenched fists
Pulverizing the rocks

One In Ten

Aphrodite abused her might
Pushing mortal men
To try and try again
Adoration for one in ten
Your chance was when
Cupid knew no end
On Earth, but never again
Of gods and mortal men
One in ten
A chance at odds
To love again

Buddha shone his light
Exposing mortal men
They scattered when
Enlightenment humbled one in ten
Centuries have passed
A century more, but never again
Of scorn and immoral men
One in ten
A chance at odds
To breathe again

Jesus stepped up from life's abyss
Leaving mortal men
Hearts drained of passion
But one in ten
Your chance was when
Crowds gathered then
His body hung on the cross, but never again
Of time and immortal men
One in ten
A chance at odds
To live again

My Perspective

The world full of impotent men
Patriarchs modifying nature's seeds
Persisting to build fires
To burn down the pillars of heaven
God should spit on them
Shouldn't he?

I had some nerve
Some independent nature
Venturing away from parents
Who wouldn't sway
Either way
They sould have left me unborn
Shouldn't they?

I'm taking up arms
Against the reflection in the mirror
Forcing him out of my head
It's my perspective
That matters
Anyway

In The Guise Of Santa

Ornaments and garland
Green, silver and red
Satan's in the guise of Santa
Marveling evergreens on Christmas eve

The emptiness underneath
To be filled by him
With gifts for *well-behaved* children
Relinquishing their innocence Christmas morning
Tearing open a parade of presents
Showered by confetti
Green, silver and red

A crown of thorns upon his head
Long forgotten
Begotten, Christ will receive
No Gold, Frankincense, or Myrrh
No wise men or star of Bethlehem

Just Satan in the guise of Santa
Moving ahead
Past Christ and His bloodshed
Decieving generations in a frenzy of
Green, silver and red
Their bodies left behind
Obscene, down river
Dead

How To Entertain A Group Of Pigs

I introduced myself
With a few imitated oinks
And they settled before me
With adoring smiles and twinkling eyes
Then I created balloon animals
Like a clown at a child's birthday party
But instead of animals they were humans
Yellow fat ones, blue skinny ones
Short green ones and tall red ones
A piglet's favorite was a woman
Filled with helium that lasts for days on a string
Curled at the end like its little tail
I dared not cast pearls before them
They'd have trampled them under their feet
And turned and rend me
I casted my voice instead
Singing *Jack and Jill*
They twirled and swinged
And snorted along

When I got tired, I created a mud pit
And they dove right in
Entertaining themselves

I Should Have Written A Haiku

Be With Me

Waltzing with death
Rising from love's depth
Reborn at each breath
Given our daily bread

Be with me
Heartbreaks
Bleeding the rose its red

The future is now
The past is in the wake of the moment
Thoughts of those gone
Fortifying memories in our heads

Be with me
Sunlight
Gilding the rose its red

Uprooted, dehydrated
Wilting low at the stems
Nature's tears are shed

Be with me
A mourner
Eulogizing the rose its red

Pages to be read
Over and over
Again and again

Be with me a poet
Imbuing the rose its red

Waltzing with death
Rising from love's depth
Reborn at each breath
Given our daily bread

Be with me the heartbeats
Bleeding the rose its red

Leaven

Mother's Favorite

Departure From This Darkroom

You're a primitive fool
Playing by the rules
Beaten by the apparition
Of your mirrored ghoul
Digging for jewels
With primitive tools
Fashioned by the fame
Of Hollywood mules
Neglecting to heed
The dawn of a new day
Ushered on in blind desire
Anticipating departure
From this darkroom
Like a rose
Waiting to bloom

Key Of Knowledge

Go within
Find yourself
Contained in heartbeat
As midnight is
Contained in moonlight

Remain within
The wisdom
That you are meant
For so much more
Than the desire for
External validation

"Woe unto you, lawyers! for ye have taken away the key of knowledge: ye entered not in yourselves, and them that were entering in ye hindered."
-Luke 11:52

My Two Sons
For Nicholas & Alexander

My two sons call out my inner child
And we construct cloud nine
I no longer expect my father to return
Here with waist-high men
In all life's time
Legacies to my bloodline

My two sons pitch in for childhood's redesign
I no longer wonder how my father's inner child
Fell to his demise
Here with whippersnappers right as rain
In all life divine
Lengthening my lifeline

My two sons journey out into the sunshine
I no longer wonder why my father cut his inner child's strings
Before his playtime
Here with heirs to fantasies
In all life has to define
Indulging in dreams and fairytale rhyme

My two sons befriend my inner child
And we enjoy fine wine from childhood's grapevine
I no longer expect my father to return
Here with waist-high men
In all life's time
Legacies to my bloodline

Middle Finger

"Tell your father he's a piece of shit," my mother said
So, I said it when he came up from the basement that night
After an inummerable amount of sips of scotch
And I added the middle
Finger
For good measure

My father said nothing
Just beat pices of shit out of me
And when he was satisfied
I was barely breathing
He made his way back down to the basement
I mangaed to give him the middle
Finger
Again

Lit By Your Face

Same Name As A Dog

When you bear the same name as a dog
You stick your head out a second story window
And annoyingly, but attentively look down at children
Calling out, "Sonia!"
Then you suffer the embarrassment
Of the children yelling up,
"Not you, the dog."

In Visible Forms

In visible forms
Four rivers flow
Through depths of atmosphere
A breeze begins to blow
Manifested souls
In crisp darkness
Enjoy the stars
Lucid in dreams
Out of ordinary
Wrapping the night in sunlight
Ascending heaven's heights
Breathing the breath of life
Objects of God's unconditional love
In visible forms
Four rivers flow
Through depths of atmosphere
A breeze begins to blow

Blue Trail

Hiking the blue trail
Under a blue sky
I stop, stare
God's fingers
Through nature's hair
A butterfly dances in the air
Past a chipmunk, past an ant
Taking a moment to consider me
Listening
To all that I've been missing
A bumble bee buzzes in the air
Waving the forest trees to and fro
Past a bull frog, past a cntipede
Taking a moment to consider me
In fine detail
I continue
Under a blue sky
Hiking the blue trail

Caricature

On creation's canvas
God composes a firmament
A sun with blaring rays
A lonely white cloud
Straying in the blue

Down below
With the feature rich countenance
Of a troubadour
He composes an imperfect man
Staring at a lonely white cloud
Straying in the blue

Pinocchio

A puppet on lowly strings
Pulled by television
Channel surfing desperatly
Like Pinocchio
Wanting to be
A real
Boy

Monday Mornings Are Stressful For My Baby Daughter

Refusal To Take Cover

Truth is absolute
Emnating from aroused breaths
Escaping our tongue kiss
Closer to heaven
The further we flee from hell
You are an image of God
A force of nature
A looming tsunami
And I refuse to take cover

One Must Write

One must write
Because they feel emotion
Unconditionally loving
Ones who cannot
A rose in their grip
Thorns clipped from the stem
For fear of bleeding
One will always fear bleeding
Listening to prophets
Recite scriptures
Of snakes and knowledge of good and evil
Disregarding a head full of ghosts
Anticipating breath
To achieve heartbeat for bleeding
One will want to feel they're bleeding
Unconditionally loving
Ones who cannot
Feeling emotion
Writing

Suffering A Spiritual Being

Suffering a spiritual being
Preparing the body
For eternal rest, listening for
The last word of God
Before expulsion from Eden
In physical form
Illogically descriptive
Love drawn from within
Regretful of original sin
Suffering a spiritual being

Leather Jacket

In Memoriam Thich Quang Duc
died by self-immolation in North Vietnam 11 June 1963

"Before closing my eyes and moving towards the vision of the Buddha< I respectfully plead to president Ngo Dinh Diem to take a mind of compassion towards the people of the nation and implement religious equality to maintain the strength of the homeland eternally. I call the venerable, reverends, members of the sangha and the lay Buddhists to organize in solidarity to make sacrifices to protect Buddhism."
-Quang Duc's last words documented in a letter he had left.

I learned of your self-immolation, Duc
Listening to *Killing in the Name*
By Rage Against the Machine
A cropped photograph of you burning
Is their album cover
It's an incomprehensible image, you
Sitting in equanimity
As violent flames consume your body
Protesting religious injustice during the Vietnam war
I thought of Christ and how he
Did not come to this earth to show
How special he was, but to show how special we are
Then I thought of the heathens who came
To your homeland
Inverting Christ's message
Making you get on yoour knees to some pastor
To get saved
You know the heathens, Duc, of course we all do
The heathens who gave the world the bikini, sewing machine
And hot air balloon
The heathens who gifted the United States
The Statue of Liberty
The heathens who colonized your homeland
Like pathogens
Giving the Vietnemese
An ultimatum; convert to catholicism or longer matter
The heathens who gave shots and death
And decimated villages

Buddhism was a potential threat
To the heathens imperial rule, as you know, Duc
When Buddhists adhered to their dharmas
And remained united, enabling them
To withstand persecution
But when factions of Buddhists abandoned their dharmas
It weakened them and made them
Susceptible to being crushed by oppressors
The former raised the consciousness of
The Vietnamese people
Awakened their Buddhas withing and
In 1949, the heathens recognized
The establishment of an independent
"State of Viet Nam" under the control of
Former Vietnamese Emperor Bao Dai

Too many cooks in the kitchen, Duc
The United States officially recognized
Bao Dai's government
But after Mao Zedong's Chinese Communists
Defeated the Nationalists Kuomintang
In 1950, China and the Soviet Union
Recognized Ho Chi Minh as Viet Nam's
Legitimate leader
So began the United States providing Bao Dai's
Government and French forces with military
Advisors and weaponary
But no matter the superior military hardware
Ho Chi Minh's resistive forces used guerlla warfare
To succesfully wear down the French
The two sides arranged peace talkls in
The spring of 1954
But before such talks took place
The French were finally defeated after the battle
Of Dien Bien Phu
Viet Nam was now free and independant
Of direct *foreign control*

Here's the kicker, Duc
Viet Nam became dividedagain as negotiations

From France, the US, China, the Soviet Union
And Viet Nam agreed to divide the nation in half
At the 17th parallel
The communists took control of the north
And the nationalists took control of the south

Devout Catholic leader Ngo Dinh Diem
With the oppresive polocies of the French
And supported by the United States
As a reliable ally
Bgean arresting and torturing Buddhist Monks
Political offices were only granted to Catholics
Foreign aid only distributed to Catholics
Land was allocated to Cathloics

One, Two, Three Tubes Of Blood

The phlebotomist
Pressed her cold, latex fingers
Against my exposed limb
Identifying the perfect vein
I winced
As a butterfly needle pierced
Into my bloodstream

Counting the tubes of blood
One, two, three
Then, as the phlebotomist pulled the butterfly needle
From an imperfect vein
I wondered of all my days
How many more my spirit
Would enjoy this human experience

Inner Guide

Inside the fitness center
By his master's side
Is this shining coat
Golden Retriever
A pair eyes for a man
Destitute of vision
Skillfully feeling for the pin
To up the resistance of a
Weight machine

When he has fatigued
His biceps
The Golden Retriever
Will lead him to his next
Exercise

I epiphanize
Losing my own sight
Allowing my intuition
To lead me
To my creator

Sunrise On The Shore

In this meager life
I feel what Adam and Eve felt in Eden
When God's presence filled their every pore
With my feet planted firmly in the sand
I witness a sunrise on the shore

Not from television
Or a calendar in the bookstore
But from the edge of the universe
I attend a sunrise on the shore

Existing as I never knew
I could before
A miracle, a ray of light
The sunrise on the shore

In this temporary life
I feel what Adam and Eve felt in Eden
When God's presence filled their every pore
With my footprints washing away in the sand
I witness a sunrise on the shore

Desire

I need recognition when I am nobody
Shivering cold I need the gatekeepers of death
To trust that I will ask to let me in
I need to exist as me I need you
I need I need to know I am no one but your only
I need to see me through I need to say
My last words
I love you
I need you to hear me

As Their Creator Did

Through the unexpected darkness
Of a wet cave
Adam explored Eve
Deeper and deeper
Abandoning a piece of himself
Within her

Acknowledging the life-form within
Eve delighted in the production
Of a separate existence
A tiny drum beat within the confines
Of unconditional love

And upon the suffering of childbirth
Eve acknowledged Adam's sympathy
Then on the sight of their newborn
They remembered the forbidden bite
Of that tempting fruit
And redefined themselves with the knowledge
Of composing life
As their creator did

Hello, Hello Again

On a sh-boom bone-chilling winter's day
I'm writing this in a coffee lounge
As a song from a Batista's soundtrack plays overhead

Life could be a dream sweetheart
Hello, hello again

The tune is most likely playing in your head now
That 1954 doo-wop
Or what they're calling now
Traditional pop

They're always calling things this
And telling us that
Lining their pockets
With our hard-earned profits

Oh oh dip a dibby dobby dip
Life could be a dream

On a sh-boom bone-chilling winter's day
I'm writing this in a coffee lounge
With spring just around the corner
Waiting to make your dreams come true
Sweetheart

Calling Out

Summer's fading
Falling in the colors of Autumn
Leaves
I stay
Battling the season's demons
Under the gray skies
Of old man Winter
Carried away
Calling out, "Returnning sunof Spring
Tell me I'm on the upswing
Show me paradise is now
And forever."

Under The Big Top

The world is spawning
Clowns and acrobats
Entertainning their egos
Performing feats
Of intellectual dexterity
Dazzled by the past
Where everything
Happens too fast
High diving
Into pools of fear
Pretending to know what heartache is for
Offending the tamers of opposing perceptions
Walking the tightropes of duality
Maintaining balance with a strong core
Paralleled feet
And no safety net

Not Eating The Pig

I attended this party once
Where the main meal
In a large, muddy pen
Had this twinkle in its eye
That said he was privy the man in overalls walking into the pen
Would take his life
So, he entertained the patronizing crowd
Running this way, that way
Snorting, his floppy ears, flopping
He glanced at me
Influencing some primordial emotional reaction
My heart skipped
As the man in overalls
Ended the show with a bullet to the meals head
The crowd cheered as it rang out
Then the meal was hoisted up by its hind legs
And while suspended in mid-air
It writhed like a criminal hanging from the gallows
As the man in overalls slit its throat
The meal was then roasted for hours
And when it was time to eat
Everyone ate the meal
Except its head
Alone on the buffet table
With a toasted complexion
And an apple in its mouth
Looking really tired
And detached

The Earthwroms Were Never Heard

To demenstrate redemtion
The earthworms surfaced on fertile ground
Congregating in the calm before the strom
Then the rain fell
And the winds howled
And the earthworms held eachother tight
As a storm ensued
And a storm soon subsided
And the earthworms were never heard
Calling out to men that they were all one
As the worm-eating Robins, Wrens, and Woodcocks
Feasted

Story To Tell

Everyone's a story to tell
Writers at contrasting vantage points
In crossfire
Round after round
Watching souls abandon their pierced apparatuses
Riding the wind into forever

Everyone's verse
Of angels soliciting
Their wings for a prayer of repentance
Fragile bodies on and off again
Until there's no longer a need for a savior

Everyone's attentive
To what holds them back
Primitive beasts naive to time
Temples crumbling
Into dust
Repalcing the Garden of Eden with a concrete jungle

Everyone's a story to tell
Writers at contrasting vantage points
Like homeless men standing on highway exits
With their memoirs written out on cardboard
In large black letters
For the world to read

Everyone's a story to tell

Panic And Pain

I am the tall oak
Housing a massive bee hive
I am its myriad guards

I am the sunflower's bloom
The nectar, the honey
The Queen

I am the boy
Naively batting the hive
With an oak stick

I am the swarm of stingers
The panic
And the pain

Breaking Bread

Zen

Yoga studios
Are overbooked
With aspiring monks striving
To convince the world they're Zen
By snapping selfies of themselves
In contorted positions

The truth of the matter is
To convince the world they're Zen
One must be in every position
But visible
Like God

Territorial Geese
For Alexander

On the shore of the Hudson River
A boy and I watch a pack of geese
Yap their beaks and hiss
Competing for water territory
Their long necks crane
As the boy lifts a pebble from the ground
Draws back his arm like a major league pitcher
And casts it into the water
Causing the geese disperse in a frenzy
The boy yelling out,
"Beat it
"This is my river!
Right Dad?"

The Stranger

She suddenly lost her footing
On a patch of ice
Nine months pregnant
With her ninth child
In the middle of winter
I stared useless
Frozen as she sat stranded on the ice
Preserving her breath for the push
When a stranger turned the corner
Of Church Street
Assessing my inadequacy
He held out his hand and lifted my mother
With the care of a saint
I stared in awe at 12 years old
Her third child
Thanking the stranger
As he wisped out like a puff of smoke
My mother and I
Trekking the remaining three blocks
To the hospital
Where I heard her
Condemned by original sin to labor a bastard child
I wished the stranger would
Turn the corner into the waiting room and hold out his hand
I'd be lifted from the floor into his embrace
And he'd be my father

The Imprint Of A Bird In The Sky

All of a sudden I find myself on the cusp of mid-life
Youth a fleeting memory
Found now in my two teenage sons
And year old daughter
And I need them to know that
The soul is the most important *thing* in this physical world
It's the soul that vanishes into emptiness
Like the imprint
Of a bird in the sky

In A Mirror

There's a boy in a mirror
Craving his creator's reflection
Forgetting to manifest light
In the dark
All torn up
An image of Jesus' miracles

He's always on the go in his dreams
All the time
The boy's sleeping
All his days away

Longing for stability
All the time
The boy's aching to hear
The silence
Between raindrops

Craving his creator's reflection
Forgetting to manifest light
In the dark
All torn up
In a mirror
The boy's unable to recognize
The image of Jesus' miracles

How Much I Love You

For Amy

I waited for my grandmother
In the lobby of the old folk's home
As she listened in the rec room
With her contemporaries
Dauber poised above her tickets
The man at the ball machine calls out I66
And I added another six
Counting the number of the beast
Which is also the number of man
Then the man at ball machine called out B7
And I thought of God, my guardian angels
And I thought mostly of you
And how much I love you
As grandma won the jackpot
Calling out in youthful praise,
"BINGO!"

No Place To Hide

Calamities televised
No escape from the camera's eye
Those barren suddenly pray
To a God they've always denied
I carry no burden
No pity, no pride
There's no place to hide
Unredemtion's televised
No escape from the camera's eye
Those bearing no fruit suddenly pray
To a God they've always denied

Undone (The Sweater Poem)

The sweater you're sporting has been
Strategically knitted over your lifetime
By family
Friends
Enemies
Television programs
Social media
Et cetera
Et cetera

Let me destroy the sweater
Hold the thread
As you walk away
Watch you indoctrination unravel
You'll soon be naked
Lying on the floor
Undone

Wing Stop
For Ryleigh

The dead birds
At Wing Stop
In their afterlife
Will never understand
The patrons
In line
Stinking of marijuana
Itching to satiate their munchies
With the dead birds
Killed before
With no chance of ever
Taking flight

All Away

All the worry, all the stress
Even my last breath
Until there's nothing left
I'm giving it all away

All the judgments of death
All the observations of art

Organized piles
Of time spent loving those who hate
Of verse written to understand my fate
Grab a box, stand in line
I'm giving it all away

All the thoughts of existence
All the dreams of kingdom come

Heavy piles
Of days without sun
Of nights searching for the one
First come, first served
I'm giving it all away

All the smiles. All the debt
Even my last breath
Until there's nothing left
I'm giving it all away

Meet Me

Meet me in black and white
Like Humphrey Bogart and Ingrid Bergman
In Casablanca
With no expectations
Under moonlight
Meet me with a compromised immune system
Love sick
For my remedy
Meet me in the eye of the storm
With chaos
Surrounding us
Meet me under the old oak tree
Amidst the stream
Deep-rooted
Meet me in an endless life
Beyond the grave
Above sunlight
In that infinite dimension
Where time and space
Hold no limits
Meet me in old fashion
Like we've never met
Before

The Snap Of The Rodent's Neck

Grandma couldn't have the rodent
Rummaging for crumbs and defecating
On the kitchen counters anymore
God only knows at 95
What type of ending she'd endure
If the rodent were to appear in her sight
Like an elephant Grandma drove herself crazy
With the thought of it *crawling up her trunk*

So, I set the trap
And the next morning
Just after a sip of coffee
There was a death
The volume of the morning news with political views
Propaganda, disease and war
Were too loud to hear the snap
Of the rodent's neck

I Imagined Being A Third Grade Music Teacher

I imagined being
A third grade music teacher
Instructing my students
To ready their recorders
For familiarization
I imagined the
Ponderous children
With clumsy fingers
And innocent breath
Play their recorders in sync
In wretched noise
I imagine this
The way of Zen

I Forgive

I forgive the host of the party for getting me drunk
Before the other guests arrived, I forgive the poet for writing
Then ripping the page in two, I forgive the old man on the
Corner for ignorantly abandoning his youth without regret
I forgive Coca-Cola for shaping the jolly character
We know today as Santa Claus
I forgive Saint Nick, I forgive my father
I forgive the Virgin Mary, I forgive my mother
I forgive the bully for pushing me to the floor
I forgive the rich, I forgive the poor
I forgive God, I forgive the Devil
I forgive the children for the games they love to play
I forgive my next-door neighbor, I forgive my sister
I forgive the last rain drop of the storm, I forgive my brother
I forgive the cafe owner for closing on Mondays
Providing me no place to write
I forgive poetry, I forgive prose
I forgive the daisy, I forgive the rose
I forgive you forgiving me
I forgive the young man for being ignorant
Of his impermanence of this human experience
I forgive the host of the party for kicking me out
Before the other guests overstayed their welcome
I forgive her for not leaving the party when I got kicked out
And overstaying her welcome
I forgive the angels, I forgive the demons
I forgive the Garden of Eden, I forgive original sin
I forgive Adam, I forgive Eve
I forgive the dying, I forgive the heart bared on my sleeve
I forgive itself, I forgive yourself
I forgive oneself, I forgive myself

When I Grow Up

I Prayed

I prayed for God to inspire me
He sent two sons
For me to love and teach
And admire for all my days

I prayed for God to expose me
He unfolded the universe
Clouds dissipated
The sun shone so bright
I became
Spirit

I prayed for God to forgive me
He opened his arms
Nature restored me
Branches of trees reached out
And embraced me

I prayed for God to walk with me
Christ descended the stairway to heaven
In the dead of night
He pulled back the veil
And stepped over to my side

A Gorilla Escaped From The Zoo

They graduate the universities
And on their walls
In heavy, elaborate frames
They hang proof
Validating their one trick
Their only tool for every obstacle
Their one way out of any argument
In absence of original thought
With egotistical authority
They attack anyone who questions their supremacy
Parroting professional opinion
Entering lecture halls worldwide
Beating their broad chests in fierce debut
Like a gorilla escaped from the zoo

As Below, So Above

Dark roast rises in relaxed fragrance
A swell of voices fill a coffee lounge
Vibrating conversations
Of cosmic consciousness
Shinning sunlight radiantly
Through the lounges windows
Illuminating the faces of the patrons
In a fanatical replica
Of the saints and angels of heaven
Here on earth

Soft Kiss

As birds compete
In morning song
Sunrise penetrates
The bedroom window's
Garments

Our cuddled knot
Securing us
To each other
Through the night
Is unbound

And with a nutritious
Soft kiss
We break fast

The day
Has begun
We have
Just begun

From Heartbeat

Love
Originates
From heartbeat

I know
Because I've spent time
Alone
In a void
Me
A nobody
A nothing

Until
She ripped through
The void
Which I was in

That vast emptiness was no match
For her heartbeat
Pounding me into existence

My own heart
Beating
I beheld her

And
I love her

Back Down

I was high this morning
Above it all

Tiptoeing to the rhythm
Of my lover's heartbeat
In the stratosphere
Over my lover's dreams
Recognizing myself as a daybreak sun beam
Emanating from the source
Of my lover's creator
A weightless gladiator

I was high this morning
Above it all

But I've come back down
For my lover's kiss
I always
Come back
Down
For my lover's
Morning kiss

The Weight Of Mankind's Wickedness

Mankind's participants are useless
Large and lifeless
The weight of their wickedness
Pins them down to broken promises
Confused and conditional
Their memory lapses deem them
Incapable of learning the creator's unconditional love
As he remains mute on their desires
Formless, immaterial consciousness
Under the weight of mankind's wickedness
He remains useless

At 44

I stopped celebrating the holidays
Sick of self righteous caroling in the streets to make
Ends meet
To hell with what the world considers holy days
And to heaven for the dog on all fours
At 44
Barking, barking, barking
Bitching about not being young anymore
Then hoarsely whimpering
For unconditional love

The Deepest Love Of My Life
For Amy

Poetry destined us to meet
At that corporate
Coffee shop
Three years ago
You know, the one with the
Siren
That mysterious nautical
Figure
Calling out
Like her heart
Calling out to mine
As she sat down
Full-bodied with a dreamy aroma
Like the anniversary blend
Double shot of espresso
I shot back
Falling into the deepest love
Of my life

Basement Apartment

Down here, I know the lord has gained some weight
His heavy footsteps strain
Heaven's hardwood floors
More and more I think the sky is going to fall

Up there, I know the lord is comfortable
I can hear him take dehumidified breaths
Opening his shades
To let sunlight flood his smile

Down here, the lord's toilet flushes
Washed dishes and candlelight baths
Drain through the pipes
Where adorable little mice
With midnight eyes
Startle me
Startling them

Up there, the lord's three dogs
Stampede through paradise
With their untrimmed paw nails
Scraping against heaven's hardwood floors
When they lay down
Wagging their tails
I can hear my time running out

Down here, the lord forgets I exist
Except on the 1st of the month
When he opens the gates of heaven
And heavy foots it to my door
Requesting another month's rent

Decide

Decide love, decide hate
Decide red, decide blue
Decide me, decide you
Decide insecurity, decide debt
Decide a helping hand, decide an abusing fist
Decide you look like a poet, a novelist, a writer
What you have to do is
Decide life, decide death
Dammit
Make a decision

Honey Bee

It seems that the honey bee
Has mis-taken my cup
Of green tea
For the last flower of the season
Landing on its lid and sucking up
Its nectar
Flying off to impress his Queen
Then dying off

Poetry

Poetry is amateur days of youth
A refuge for prematurely orgasmic verse
Poetry is an expression of the stars
Poetry is insanity, poetry is metaphorically omnipresent
Poetry is figuratively benevolent
Poetry is a quality of being, poetry is the state
You were to be in, poetry is the depths of love
Poetry is an invitation for the prodigal son to return
Home

From Above

Gazing from above
It looks as if the people
Of the world were productive
But when you stand
On the ground below
It's clear
The people of the world
Have made a huge mess
Refusing to take on the
Responsibility of
Cleaning up

Not Wanting To Sleep

We live eternities
In the blink of an eye
Still, at life's conclusion
We will beg for the beginning
Like a child not wanting to sleep
Pleading to be read a bedtime story after its end
Again and again

Acknowledgments

I would like to thank the following people for their encouragement and support. Without them, this book would not have been possible.

Nicholas Olsen
Alexander Olsen
Bill Webber
Jane Harries
Michael Glassman
Eva-Maria Araujo - RIP

www.ingramcontent.com/pod-product-compliance
Ingram Content Group UK Ltd.
Pitfield, Milton Keynes, MK11 3LW, UK
UKHW030348050125
453025UK00006B/67

9 781733 545075